Iridescent self

Yailyn Cortez

BookLeaf Publishing

India | USA | UK

Presentation by *BookLeaf Publishing*

Web: www.bookleafpub.com

E-mail: info@bookleafpub.com

ISBN: 9789363309708

First edition 2024

I dedicated this to my past self, I have become the person I needed and wanted within my life and to anyone who is on the path to self discovery and soul nourishment. I am cheering everyone on because I know how hard the path is and how difficult it is. Sometimes on this journey I want to run but I can't so I am forced to deal with myself anyways. It is truly something one has to dedicate and commit to. I truly applaud everyone who has felt this way and overcome this way. We don't congratulate ourselves enough and we should.

ACKNOWLEDGEMENT

I want to thank everyone who has experienced life with me, I truly couldn't be the person I am today without them. Good or bad, I became the person I am because of those experiences I lived in and saw many different lives and perspectives. I've shed different versions of myself because of this, which in turn allowed me to come back into myself after running time and time again seeking a foreign element outside myself. Tuning back into myself was the most profound discovery I have ever come across. It's all within me and in the end, I was blocking and running while searching for myself. The journey is tough and less traveled but it is indeed the most rewarding. I also want to thank BookLeaf Publishing for giving me the opportunity to join the 21 Day Writing Challenge. The opportunity and dream of expanding myself is now coming into fruition and I am given the chance to showcase myself.

PREFACE

I wrote this to inspire myself to transcend internal and external expectations of me. Originally I thought I had to be very seasoned in the writing and literature world to begin to even have the audacity to write a book. I soon came to realize I was limiting myself, writing a book was thought it would be such a high and honorable leap. I read books in my childhood years that gave me the spark to want to bring my world into this world. When I say my world, I mean what I create in my head, ideas, visions, likes, stories and scenarios in order for people to really see me. I lived in my head a lot, I found a sense of self through that and through that I was strong in who I was. Giving me such a light and bright upbringing. I loved to write for others because it gave me the feeling of accomplishment when I see the look on someone's face after reading my old work. It was a sense of wonder, joy and a newfound inspiration for life and self. I loved seeing that in other people and helping them realize what life can be and what it can feel like. Even if it's not there, it's like we are playing pretend as kids and still having more fun than the average person going on vacation.

Escape

Most people run from themselves without
knowing it, it is an unconscious action that one
does,
I see it everywhere.
People numbing, running and dulling their lives
away looking for what sparks their life.
Yet to their dismay, it is only a temporary
fleeting feeling.
All of these are unconscious actions.Sleeping to
eating to drinking to friends to gaming
It's everywhere I look in life.
Each interaction I see people escaping their
reality that they have created themselves through
experiences, people and the moment.
I have come to this realization and at that
moment a chain snapped.
I was free
Free from what you might say?
Free from unawareness.
Becoming more aware of my actions and the
world around me is scary.
I really began to see what I do, what I say and
what I consume.
Consumption is a big thing, you know the phrase
you are what you eat

And this comes down to all sorts of consumption
Whether it's the thoughts you feed yourself, the
media you watch, the music you listen and even
the people around you.
I have always disliked the term consumers for
some reason in high school.
I had a passion and would try to explain why I
hated it to my peers.
At the time I didn't really know but iI came to
realize that deep down I was also a consumer.
I was restricting myself through consumption
and no production..
This reminded me of my biology class I took in
high school.
I remember learning there was 2 types of
categories in this world
One being consumers and the other being
producers.
To produce is to create and give life to others.
To consume blindly without much thought is just
a way of coming into being.
I guess I realized I've been too afraid to come
into myself.
Doing this would require me to go after myself
and chase after myself with the results being
more nerve wracking.
Whether I rose or fell, I knew it would hit me
hard.

The thing about life is that, that in itself is the
main reason why we live.
We live to go through life seamlessly whether
we fell or not, it's the fact that we still had that
fire within us to keep going.
Fire is what lights up life.
Without light there's no life.
Our eyes can only see less than 1% of life
And with how intricate, complex yet beautiful
life is from different angles, knowing there's
way more to life is a motivator.
Imagine all of the great things we can't see, hear,
experience yet the life we CAN see is more than
enough for us as human beings is beyond what
we can comprehend.
The more challenging the more rewarding as
they say.
Finding and reaching myself was the hardest yet
most rewarding thing I have ever done in my
life, for it was within me to really grasp and go
after what I want and knowing that I had forever
me to fall back on.
For you can never abandon yourself for you are
always there for you no matter what.

State of love

Lots of people idealize this and search for a love
greater than themselves.
This can be manifested in multiple ways for
various types of people,
A love of people, experiences, wealth and as
most come to know that special person you hold
close and dear.
Though love is a personification of love within
oneself.
Most fail to realize that and go through life
searching for that missing piece they don't know
they need.

A girl like me, has once been this way,
For I have thought I already loved myself.
Though it was only conditionally.
If I did well enough, if I went beyond, if I
appeared a certain way ect.
Most times I seeked it outside of me,
Looking for it in forms of validation through
academics, socially and through others who.
I thought this was enough and didn't think much
of it.
Until I fell into a hole of self induced spiral
downward.

I was picking parts of me to become perfect.
I was my biggest critic because I seeked
validation and love through others.
Though when hitting the bottom of the hole, the
only way from there is up.
In which I did.

Over time I slowly came to love and accept
myself.
The shadows, the parts I rejected of myself.
I cried over this believe it or not.
I thought
How could I reject that part of me, or any for
that matter?
That part of me just wanted to be accepted and if
no one were to accept her, she would not be
recognized.

I learned how to accept my flaws and love them
for who I am, truly.
Without the validation of others I began to really
radiate from the inside out due to this.
Opportunities were flowing seamlessly and life
felt less restricted.
Like the whole time I wasn't truly loving and
accepting myself it felt like as if I had a pair of
jeans way to tight,
And loving myself was like wearing a flowy
skirt with lots of space.

I was embracing myself in vulnerability, my
femininity, my past and my what might be
perceived as ugly.

All of me is beauty and love in which that is all I
see in life.
Life is like a piece of artwork, a deep and
twisted love story within itself.
For all in life is love and everything is a just but
a mere facade separating you from it.
Falling into myself was like surrendering to it
all.
Surrendering and letting life take the wheel.
Flowing with life and seeing where it takes me.
Nothing has been as freeing and light as going
with life's flow.
I stopped caring and put myself first.

I deserve to put myself first, since I am all I
really have at the end of my life.
So I should love, accept and enjoy my time here
being my body.
To be selfish in self-love is selfless

Yin to Yang

Life has lots of highs and lows
Without it, it can't really be labeled as life.
The highs and lows are polar opposites of the
same spectrum.
Without the lows we can't appreciate the highs
And with the highs going just as they came, so
does the lows
Time is the reason for this
Without time we can't not go forward with our
lives
Time does not wait for us, it goes and life keeps
on going
There is always something to be looking forward
to somewhere in the world
Someone can be experiencing their highs while
you can be living in a present low.
Everyone has their time
We can only guess and not accurately predict the
future.
The only thing we can do is live in the moment.
To live in the moment is to soak up the
experience you are currently living in order to
gain clarity on how to move forward with life.
Clarity is a beautiful sight of lenses that finally
give you a fresh breath of air after being in the

mind space of the overstimulating world of
today.
It is the very thing that allows us to push
ourselves into something great.
With clarity, the veil of illusion falls and we
soon begin to accelerate forward.
As we see, the very thing blocking us from our
own very success was us in the very end.
A breakthrough in our personal development
allows us to set a different base bar.
Once we reach a new conclusion we can never
go back.
The only way is up afterall.
The only way out is to keep going.
And with time and life, it doesn't stop for
anyone
Not one soul
To live is to experience life and life flows
endlessly and freely with infinity resolutions.
It's in our capability to choose what we really
want for ourselves.
Not just us on the surface like what we think we
want but underneath with enough contemplation.

Self sabotage?
Negative self beliefs?

Fear of being seen?
Fear of success?

How could the very things we want be
something we run from at the same time.
Perhaps it's the predicament of climbing so high,
that the fall would cause so much hurt and
sorrow.

To risk is to really live.
To love is to be vulnerable enough to risk your
heart
To gain is to invest your time and hard work
To improve is to discipline yourself through
countless tests and hardships one has to go
through.

Hard work is admirable
It's admirable because it signals to the other
person about how passionately and how
stubborn it was to reach that goal.
Chasing dreams is admirable these days.

It truly is, most people tend to stick with
comfortability and never rise to their highest
self.

Their highest self would be the bestest self they
can think of, no doubt.
The only thing restricting the thought of the
result would be action taken towards it whether
it's small or big, it is progress.
The best investment an individual would make
in their lifetime for the highest good of them all
would be investing in oneself.

Leo's Courage

The courage and sheer strength it takes to hold
yourself accountable
is very commendable.

It would be a great shame to not take pride in
our own self work
The art of self mastery is one that is often looked
over and forgotten
Self mastery is refining and enhancing the parts
of self in order to be most elevated
When life becomes hard and overbearing, one
can forget about their self which is the greatest
lost one can suffer

How can one sustain others if they aren't secure
at the base of themselves.
Life is within our control and when we spin out
of control this can happen.

Is it the sacrificial act of love?
Complete selflessness?
Self neglect?
Emotional avoidant?
Love comes out on top each and every time

We love too much outside ourselves; we forget
we yearn to meet that spark within ourselves to
attain and embody self love.

The epitome of love is the journey to self love.
For love outside ourselves is merely a reflection
of us
Our hopes, dreams, wishes and traits we limit
ourselves to reach.

To be purely seeking an incredible love that isn't
within us is just running from something that
was there alone.
It was just that we needed to recognize, see it
and accept it to truly love ourselves.
This path in life is a hard , treacherous one but
one that is so rewarding.
It truly is rewarding.

Everyday it is a bliss to wake up to yourself
Not only that, we also look after and watch
ourselves in person.
Even subconsciously, we are shielded so
desperately in a way we won't hurt ourselves.
Ego is manifested but it only separates from
feeling and expressing love.
Teaching ourselves it is okay to love and it is
okay to do those things that hurt us in the past.

It can show up as running from things we love
out of fear.

Which is such a devastating love story in itself.
Though with enough time, patience and self
understanding it all comes back together
beautifully like a miracle.
Through the time it takes to nurture oneself is
one that is as common as taking time of in order
to recollect and reenergize ourselves.
Even if we think we don't need it, it is still a
great reminder.
Like that person you love dear and close to your
heart, it feels nice to know someone loves you
whether it's through acts of love, affirmation,
intimacy, gift-giving and even just the absolute
act of just spending time with that person.

A parent caring for their child would be what
one is to themselves.
Isn't it comedical for one to serve as both roles
to themselves at the same time?
It is also beautiful to know that we aren't alone
within ourselves.

Both the parent exists as the careful, watchful
and protective self and the inner child within us
that sees the world with color joy and wonder.

The Unspoken Law

Law of attraction

A phenomenon that implies you reap what you
sow.
If your expecting the worst, the outcome would
be the worst

But if your expecting the best, you'll get the
best, now
See how that changes things, instead of feeling
cursed

You can now fly and be the director of your life.
It is the mindset of embodying what you want
externally.

Why live a live full of strife
When you can attract all that you want by
merely altering yourself internally.

It is one of the laws of the universe that we all
find ourselves in
We are attracting whether we see it or not

Everyday, people don't recognize the instant
power that comes from within.
By manually taking control and directing rather
than feeling like your life is in a knot

Taking power can be as simple as manifestation.
Which is the act of assembling something out of
mind

Fueling our creations would be by relying and
bringing it into life by sole emotion
And with actively staying on the path, it all
becomes entwined.

Like a long awaited piece to the puzzle coming
together beautifully.
Except that most of the time it's not exactly what
you wanted but better.

You would think we would rather want exactly
what we think of now, but typically
Life goes on, we grow and change, that's when it
begins to matter.

The Burden of With Holding Thyself

Suppression of yourself
When acting from a place of fear
Life becomes a state of an artificial self that has
been created
That state of self is the base of the current reality
that one holds near
When coming back into authenticity it all start to
crash down when it's unrelated

I dream of a life where people can step out of
their comfort zone
Away from ego
Making most a clone
Paving the way for authenticity to replace the
standard instead of the shadow
Rather than pushing a front in order to be falsely
known

Authenticity has such a strong pull
It is magnetizing and raw
Run with that instead of living a sense of self
that makes your life dull
I swear it is a universal law

That one can use to their benefit for their
upliftment without beating yourself cruel
Hiding from a perceived flaw
When uniqueness is free and abundant where
your life is your rule

It's a path where you may tumble and stumble
Where you give and earn yourself true value
May you hold yourself true and dear
In order to be see and be clear

Hiding from shame and being shamed
Is an oppressor
Real strength, resilience and vitality to be truly
self tamed
Resulting in a place of a valid successor
One given to self in order to be a master
acclaimed

Once you breakout of that unconscious grasp
Life frees up
And begins to set in after fleeing from that clasp
Simultaneously color overflows your cup
Delayed rewards come in without an ask
A string of blockage from self that has been cut

Journey of self
Becomes a soul searching predicament
Feeling the way out of outside help

Earning the ability of discernment
Without the need to cope

Fish in Pond

Outgrowing spaces

A difficult life experience
Transformation, and improvement

I admit to having trouble letting go
Change is needed in life

To let go is to allow the process of transcending
the mundane
It's instinctive to avoid hardship

After all it's letting a piece of you to die

Awareness to no longer resonating with the old
anymore

Where staying is delaying life's requirement of
personal growth.
In the sense of the inner world and as well as the
outer

Prolonging the inevitable
An act of self-betrayal

Outgrowing a room is finding oneself isolated
The moment of realization

That the world was crumbling down all that time
Is now instantly understood

Through voluntary ignorance
The you-niverse forces acknowledgement and
action

An illusion willfully casted onto self
Fooling into perceived glee

All a desperate call to tune in
To finally meet halfway

Revitalize Life

Anew
New experiences grant me
They grant the chance to expand oneself

Sometimes you can amaze yourself as you
amaze others
It feels great

Once it's over
And you realize that you HAD climb that
mountain

It is a feeling of contentment and a sense of
pride when achieving
Through achievement the ball begins to roll
And that rolls, you keep on progressing

More mountains to overcome and more
achievements
Not only do you inspire yourself to do more but
others as they SEE what you are as a person.
Jumping that leap encourages others to do the
same
It's the greatest act of selflessness and self love.

For your coming into yourself and at the same
time encouraging others to take that leap too

Doing this grants so much more vividness to
life.
We really begin to feel, see and love life as we
achieve
It can be a personal goal, small or big.

It inspires
It's a known rule that no work in the universe is
unseen.
All work is not in vain.
It is observed and rewarded through time.

To follow one's heart and ignore reason and
logic is the highest thing you can do.
Nonconformity brings the ability to transcend

It no longer fazes to stand out and only
encourages to push on

Life is great
Life is grand
Life is giving

And, life is ever expanding
Love life so life can love you back too.
You are what you make of it

The unconscious mirrored into reality
Now you see what you can do
If you stop being so flighty
Life is ever going and ongoing

Everything changes
Everything goes
Everything flows

So just flow with what feels right and brings
contentment

Progression Rush

Thrill
The way we as humans gain a sense of self

Through the ever constant chase towards the
thrill
The thrill of it all

Why we even do what we do
And want what we want

The thrill is an electric charge to the heart of
heading after one's desire
Whatever it yearns for.
Whether it's the ever going expandment of
horizons
Or even finding love throughout life through
multiple people through yourself
Having the zeal for life is like a constant dream

It's above it all
High on the sky
And away from burdens of why

Towards self sufficiency
Towards the dreams

The ones the world told us not to do because of
how impossible it is
Every step is a step towards it
In time you'll be on your very way there

Having to keep it on
Having to hang on

Dealing and straining

To exist
To torture oneself through the hardships of the
opposite of dreams
To dream big is to live

For all we are
Is even the word, of the most high
And for that we are able to fly
Fly sky high

Potential is limitless
and we are limited by society
Only we can we ourselves from restriction
Until then, the inner you, is waiting for you to
tap in

Ready to start
And face the hardships of running towards what
everyone says it's impossible and unheard of

If only they knew how extraordinary we are

We are, our potential
That is not present until we progress

Gifted the vision of a future prophecy that can
only be fulfilled through the one that received it.
Dreams are a magical occurrence of visions we
encounter

Secret Component

Soul Searching

To travel is to live
To live is to travel

Being stranded is keeping your energy stagnant
Energy is meant to flow limitlessly and free as it
can be

Strandedness is form of self depletion

Made to move
Made to flow

Traveling in person
Traveling in thought
Traveling in spirit

A great intensity one is to realize

To expand oneself upon the world
To experience existence of something more

Learning how to expanding oneself can be
through the form of knowledge

Knowledge is something tangible
Existence is tangible

Travel brings new
The new cycles out the old
And with the old out, we can pursue

Premier Vision

Apple of an eye
Beauty
Is in the eye of the beholder
Your reality is a reflection of your mind

And your mind's eye,
Is the Intuition
of divine knowing

And what more does the divine know
Well the divine knows what we know
And we know all

For our brain can capture all
Now are we all brain or we, we

Matter of fact we are we and we are one

One to all
None to one

All can perceive
Hear
See
And choose to accept or think

Whatever we choose is the result
Thus with result is the birth of a new reality

Aka, your own little world

We are creators whatever we believe is right

At least for that moment, right?

What matter is that we believe in it with all our
heart

Now do we all have heart

Some are duller and numb than others

But all have heart

Whether it is inactive or not
It can love

Love is abundant
Love is everywhere

Beauty in love
Love in beauty

Life is love
Love is life

Lots of love
Everywhere in this world

The light rain
Touching down onto the grass

Where little life is
You may wonder how such life can be harbored
that small

All about perception,
Mindfulness
and thoughtfulness

Akin

Like
The likeness of all
What motivates

What pushes are likeness in order to be adored
With admiration, comes appreciation

It is wonderful to admire
The likeness of others,
Their inspirations
Which birth new creations
That inspire more with fuel

Fueling order to reach high
And achieve

To give life and help others dreams

For without dreams we are nothing
Nothing of monotone slaves

Slaves to external factors

That don't service the internal factor

Which is detrimental to the life force harbored
within each and everyone

Now is it light and bright?
Or is it dull and gray

To have a dream

One that lights your inner child
That brings out that smile
The one that brings you future visions of what
you can be doing

All very detrimental to the creation
Of the path one has yet to follow

All there is,
Is to go through and follow

Be the sunshine to your heart
Which will shine and radiant
And fall onto others as a light

To help others
Find their way back onto their path

Some who didn't even know they were lost

Each and everyone

No matter how small or none

It is the matter of doing

Following the heart

And dancing to the beat of it's drum

For all hearts are different
But they all love

And what's more beautiful than love itself?

It is coming back into love
The hardship that life may bring

Where we forget what it is to truly love

Love in ourself
Through passions
Hobbies
People
Nature
Creatures
Music

There's so much to love and there is so much to
life

Once one steps out the box
That society had put them in

Then they will see how abundant they really are

For we are, our source
Our source of power, pride and creation

All can be done through doing

And with the act of doing comes the act of being
in the present

Where nothing else matters past or future.

It is all in the now.

And whatever is achieved in the now
Is so impactful to your next move.

Will you keep on or will you harbor a stop

Keeping on will never be a move you regret
We move up
Through conquering our limits, fears and
expectations

It is a true breath of fresh air

One so detrimental that we didn't know we need
it
Until we reach it

Soul Slumber

Mindfully Unaware

The conscious act of the unconscious

A realm
And magical place of space and time

Where nothing seems to matter

A wonderful and beautiful escape

An escape every human being is required to do

We rest our bodies and mindfully play

In a playground and labyrinth abyss of our own
doing

Happens is what we make of it

The mental dream plane

The one where we can achieve the impossible

Who's to say we can't

We can fly

We can go far and wide

We can see
We can travel
Where we can just be

Where the colors are so vibrant
and apparent
we can't help but gleam

There's nothing that is impossible

We are our own limits,
 our own enemy and our greatest friend

We make what
Of what we will

The life is our creation
Of which our reality is tapped into

Will it stray
Will it go?

That's for ourselves to decide

Divine Force

Crushing pressure
A trait I find to be the most admirable
Is when one takes the initiative to outdo

Outdo themselves
Others
Expectations

When one makes takes destiny into their own
hands
When enough pressure is applied one
Can pass through that very boundary

 The best work is done
under pressure

Whatever the pressure is made out of
Usually comes the result of emotions
Liquid gold

Emotions are massive burst of emotion
When acted upon is like a leakage

A change happens
A change in the surrounding environment

One has to manage well
When that emotion is monitored
And directed mindfully

It creates the very essence of
A timeless piece

Why do we humans like such art?

What's so wonderful to see the result of
suffering?

It is reflected into nature

As we are

Nature breaks
to miraculously create

Like the volcano that
Erupts from the ocean

The volcano that creates land
Where land creates life

Where mother's create a Incandescent being

Where we are limitless
And filled with overflowing potential

Game of Resilience

Destiny

""Until you make the unconscious conscious,
it will direct your life and you will call it fate.",
said a world renowned philosopher.

To take matters into our own hands
To not go where energy flows

But to create a new path
One for the greater good
One for all of humanity
One for generations to come

To be as influential
And to be revolutionary

In when making such a small seemingly
insignificant change

Who knew what would be to come.

Our reality is truly dictated by our own fate
What we do in daily lives

Time watches us
What we do catches up

Whether we are rewarded
Or eventually punished

Who's to say this?

Well eventually we our own judge

We dictate and we punish and we become
What more better

Better to be

Better to become

Better of it all

We are our own greatest asset
What we make of ourselves
The greatest investment in our own lives

It truly is a world of our own
We make it how we see it

And how we see it mindfully is what it becomes

And through that we make up of little parts

To become the fruition of creation

What seemingly little minimal sparks of light
Turns into a magical formation
One, of one's doing

Solely by just believing

Quantum Oddity

Filters of the layers

To see the end
To see through it all

To see what we become and what will be

What is the inevitable and what is taken

The action of our doing
is our own undoing

To mindfully be, to just be and see

Now what will that be

To drop into self

Falling to a never ending spiral

To finally let go

Of what hold us stagnant

Where stagnancy is an illusion

Where if we're not going up

We're just loosing

Losing to who?

Time

Where no one can hide
Outdo or out run

We are all players

Players in a silly little world

It's actually quite beautiful and quite funny

If all just comes to stop
To mindfully let go
And relax, to finally catch a long breathe

To hold a breathe so long that it reaches the tips
of your toes to the back of your head

Where we are rejuvenated and revived

Where with wave of air
Takes all the muck and dirt of everyday's
holdings

Dense heavy, hard energy
That is soulbreaking to carry

Why keep playing when it is just a game

Where we can watch the game and simply be

It's easier to navigate and dictate through just
observing

Sheep are blinded
They are told to work and slave away

And or what?
To not be able to live their own

Tirelessly climbing for the value we give
ourselves

Truth is we are more valuable than we are ever
made to know

To finally achieve

Is that will make the climb halt

When will we be satisfied?

What are we starving and striving for?

We are the value we give ourselves
Found internally

Mandate and coordinate in order to gain control

Control of one's life rather than be swayed by it

That's the life of a black sheep

Self Enslavement

Addictions

I ask myself why does one run after things

Is it a high
To just live in an everyday lie?

A never ending loop of being caught within
oneself
A loop placed upon self

Where to fight is to win
And to win to gain

An invisible valuable gain
Where it will truly not fall in vain

For what we do and what we achieve is
Ever so gracefully given back to

Whether the act
It always comes back

The pressure of just wanting to
To fall in

As to why

To show how one can triumph

A never ending fight with oneself

To save and to betray your worst and greatest
enemy

The self

An neverending tale,
Tall as time and

To finally gain momentum and to finally try

To truly try
Is when we really begin to see ourselves fly

That is the truth to it all

How does one fly
When we outrank and outdo ourselves

There's no competition but the result past you
And to only to keep is to really win

How we take back our own control

To finally take that massive leap
A faithful trust
At the weight of imposing risk

We truly can achieve
What we can do

And we do with what we are
As we are

Transcending Levels

51

Breaking the algorithm

The universe is a song
As the frequencies all morph into
A massive grand piece of divine art
Beyond the comprehension of the human psyche

To follow the sole rhythm of thyself

All humans have song

We strive
Move
Sing
Dance
Inspire
Create with music

A song divinely instructed from the universe
As one is and as one does

Lead by the heart
While standing beside it, the mind
Mindfully creating
Logically refining a path onto enlightenment

The soul state of peak

When we follow the beat to our own heart
Miracles happen

A magical vast life experience

Doors magically swept open
After standing before it, searching for that key

When the key was within one
When one ventured hard and deep enough

When one acted upon the soul urge
Divinely led by the heart

Experiences are handed
Opportunities are presented

Life gets so glamorous and animated

A glorious play
When one is the author, the writer, the director
and actor

The heart's potential to reach one another
If not by mind
It is done by heart

When one is tuned into themselves
When one is clear and in living

To see life with full clarity
The clarity and space

The right mindstate to be

To be is to being
Being is what dictates what beings one is

The massive field the heart reaches when
presented in pure bliss and intention

Hue Circle

Pink

Love
A color that commonly appears in mind is pink

Pink
A controversial light element

A color that signifies lightless of life
A shade of the empowering red

A world of fun, lightheartedness and easiness
A calming softening color

What can be represented is the light feminine
A powerful component of the female aspect of
hue mans
Light beings
As we are

And with color
We can't create more

What is to create is to dwell deeper into the
comprehension of meaning

What we believe we create

Children were thought to make up things
That their imagination was to vast
Too vast for the truth it seems
But truth is stranger than fiction
That we know

In order to create, we make
We make up information
By purely gathering key parts
And seemingly put them into a case of
understanding
And what is perceived is the truth

Until proven not
Which again, we create yet again create

And so the cycle continues
A battle of one's ambition
One's might
Against all odds
But oddity seems to be the outlier and winner
As only one can win

All in a cycle and battle, a play or whatever is to
grasp
A play against the universe against the self
In deeper form

Amusement

Muse
To be loved
Is to be thought of

With all the world
And understandings of life

To take space in another's mind
Enough to create and inspire

Is to really bask in the creation of one's work
Massively admired among others when time has
past
Nostalgia does peak heart

And when we look back we see more
We see what was once great
Though it is stronger to live in the present

In that moment we were living
Not looking back or endlessly dreaming

What was done, was being
Content and intune with the present

The universal key aspect to happiness
And with true happiness comes ever flowing joy
in the present

Presenting as authentic self
And when we act from the vibration of
authenticity regardless of what we are fronting
Becomes truly magnetizing to what we are at the
moment

Repelling the inauthentic
And attaining the anew grandeur openings
With act of being authentic
A true priceless state of being

One, most can't afford
For their ego seems to hard to let go
Through all the hurt and sorrow
TIme and pressure forcing the growth of the ego

To just let go is a hard task among many
To leave behind and go forth

To go forth and propel into a new reality of
living
To thoughtfully create is to mindfully be in a
state of flow
Energy flows where attention goes

Direct your attention where you envision
yourself to be
To imagine is to dream as night as day

Imagination is your creation

Create with feeling, create with imagine
Create with loving
And create with inspiring
As many others will be led on and than inspired
As great inspires more greatness

Art is seen among the world
It is created and here by the past
The pas inspiration, envisions, pictures, thoughts
and endearing feelings

Where one can direct their energy of
overbearing passion, sentiment and thus the soul

To create with emotion displays the soul

Where our souls can't reach
We be
Where we be, we can only act from a state of
flow

When backed by false boundaries, restrictions
We forget our soul and heart

Becoming barcodes for the corporations
Not for the greater good of humanity
More like the greater good of their pockets

To fight selflessly, you are enormously rewarded
in time
Presented with mystic

Surpassing the the current understanding of what
we see, are and be

Universal Projection

Mysterious alluding facade

The different shapes, fonts, filters we see out our
eyes is just an illusion
We can choose the everafter reality

We are, where we are
Becomes unconsciously we are here
For many reasons
Mostly deeper than shallow

Each millisecond, infinite possibilities fly,
Each presenting
Infinite realities

True limitlessly being

Everything is an illusion of the reflecting
sunlight
Each projected and perceived different;y and
anew each passing moment
At each moment
A new story begins and another ends

More opportunity

Bringing forth more options to extend

The projections of light change each second with
each moment
The movement of the moment is energy